This book belongs to

THE SQUARE BEAR BOOK

MARTIN LEMAN

PELHAM BOOKS

Little Jack Horner
Sat in the corner,
Eating a Christmas pie;
He put in his thumb,
And pulled out a plum,
And said, 'What a good boy am I!'

Round and round the garden
Like a teddy bear;
One step, two step,
Tickle you under there!

Ride a cock-horse
To Banbury Cross
To see what Tommy can buy;
A penny white loaf
A penny white cake,
And a two-penny apple pie.

a song of sixpence,
A pocket full of rye;
Four and twenty blackbirds,
Baked in a pie.

When the pie was opened,
The birds began to sing;
Was not that a dainty dish,
To set before the king?

Little Robin Redbreast
Sat upon a rail;
Niddle noddle went his head,
Wiggle waggle went his tail.

Georgie Porgie, pudding and pie,
Kissed the girls and made them cry;
When the boys came out to play,
Georgie Porgie ran away.

Star light, star bright,
First star I've seen tonight,
I wish I may, I wish I might,
Have this wish I wish tonight.

Lavender's blue, dilly, dilly,
Lavender's green.
When I am king, dilly, dilly,
You shall be queen.
Who told you so, dilly, dilly,
Who told you so?
'Twas mine own heart, dilly, dilly,
That told me so.

Pat-a-cake, pat-a-cake, baker's man,
Bake me a cake as fast as you can;
Pat it and prick it, and mark it with B,
Put it in the oven for Baby and me.

Hush-a-bye, baby, on the tree top,
When the wind blows the cradle will rock;
When the bough breaks the cradle will fall,
Down will come baby, cradle and all.

Wee Willie Winkie runs through the town,
Upstairs and downstairs in his night-gown,
Rapping at the window, crying through the lock,
Are the children all in bed,
for now it's eight o'clock?

The End

PELHAM BOOKS

Published by the Penguin Group
27 Wrights Lane, London W8 5TZ, England
Viking Penguin Inc., 375 Hudson Street, New York, New York 10014, USA
Penguin Books Australia Ltd, Ringwood, Victoria, Australia
Penguin Books Canada Ltd, 10 Alcorn Avenue, Toronto, Ontario, Canada M4V 3B2
Penguin Books (NZ) Ltd, 182-190 Wairau Road, Auckland 10, New Zealand

Penguin Books Ltd, Registered Offices: Harmondsworth, Middlesex, England

First published 1991

Research and design by Jill Leman

Typeset by Pastiche, London
Printed and bound in Great Britain by William Clowes Ltd, Beccles and London

A CIP catalogue for this book is available from the British Library
Library of Congress Catalog Number 91 61348

ISBN 0 7207 2003 6